Life Cycles
Lion

Nancy Dickmann

Brown Bear Books

Published by Brown Bear Books Ltd
4877 N. Circulo Bujia
Tucson, AZ 85718
USA

and

Unit 3/R, Leroy House
436 Essex Rd
London N1 3QP
UK

© 2020 Brown Bear Books Ltd

ISBN 978-1-78121-538-8 (library bound)
ISBN 978-1-78121-565-4 (paperback)

All rights reserved. No part of this book may be reproduced, stored in a retrieval system or transmitted in any form or by any means, electronic, mechanical, photocopying, recording or otherwise, without the prior written permission of the copyright holder.

Library of Congress Cataloging-in-Publication Data available on request

Text: Nancy Dickmann
Design Manager: Keith Davis
Picture Manager: Sophie Mortimer
Children's Publisher: Anne O'Daly

Manufactured in the United States of America
CPSIA compliance information: Batch#AG/5633

Picture Credits
The photographs in this book are used by permission and through the courtesy of:

Front Cover: Shutterstock: Aurturo De Frias main, Maggy Meyer cl, Erwin Niemand bl, Stuart G. Porter tl; Interior: iStock: Steve Adams 14–15, 20br, bucky 4, Guenter Guni 18–17, 20bl, Earl Liason 6–7, Manta Photo 8–9, Maggy Meyer 4–5, Bero Serge 20tr, Stobi 16; Shutterstock: Tony Campbell 10–11, Chadha Pranav, 18–19, 20tl, Ko Grigorita 13, Andrey Dudkov 1, 18, Ilike 8, Maggy Meyer 10, 12–13, Cheryl Ann Quigley 21, tacud 6, Mogens Trolle 14.

All other artwork and photography © Brown Bear Books.

t-top, r-right, l-left, c-center, b-bottom

Brown Bear Books has made every attempt to contact the copyright holder. If you have any information about omissions please contact: licensing@brownbearbooks.co.uk

Websites
The website addresses in this book were valid at the time of going to press. However, it is possible that contents or addresses may change following publication of this book. No responsibility for any such changes can be accepted by the author or the publisher. Readers should be supervised when they access the Internet.

Words in **bold** appear in the Useful Words on page 23.

Contents

What Is a Life Cycle?................. 4
Meet the Pride 6
Lion Cubs 8
Staying Safe............................. 10
Cubs at Play............................. 12
Finding Food 14
Growing Up 16
Starting Again 18
The Life Cycle........................... 20
Fact File 21
Try It! 22
Useful Words............................ 23
Find out More........................... 24
Index 24

What Is a Life Cycle?

All animals have one thing in common. They all have a life cycle. A mother animal has babies. They grow into adults. One day they will die.

A male lion might have many young before it dies.

Mammals have a special life cycle.
The mothers make milk to feed their babies.
Lions are mammals. They follow this life cycle.

Meet the Pride

A **pride** of lions rests in the sun. The lions live in Africa. Most of them are adult females. There are a few males, and young lions, too. But soon there will be more.

Lions are the only big cats that live in groups. Tigers live alone.

One of the **lionesses** is **pregnant**. It is time for her cubs to arrive. She leaves the pride. She finds a safe, quiet place to give birth.

Lion Cubs

The **lioness** has a **litter** of **cubs**.
Most litters have two to four cubs.
The baby lions can't open their eyes.
They are small and helpless.

All mammal mothers make milk to feed their babies.

The cubs feed on their mother's milk. They grow bigger. Their eyes open. The cubs learn to walk and run.

WOW!

Lion cubs have spots when they are born. The spots fade when the cub gets older.

Staying Safe

The **lioness** must go out and find food.
She leaves the **cubs** hidden in the den.
They move to a new den every few days.
This keeps them safe from **predators**.

A lioness has sharp teeth and powerful jaws. But she can carry a cub without hurting it.

Now the cubs are eight weeks old. It is time for them to join the **pride**. The other lionesses help the mother take care of her cubs.

Cubs at Play

There are often other **cubs** in the **pride**.
They are about the same age.
The cubs spend their days playing.
They like to fight and wrestle.

The cubs are having fun. They are also learning important skills. They will need them when they start hunting. Playing helps them learn and get stronger.

Pet kittens also practice stalking and pouncing.

Finding Food

Lions only drink milk when they are **cubs**. They start eating meat when they are a few months old. Lions hunt other animals. They often catch buffalo and antelopes.

Lions hunt zebra. These stripy animals are fast runners.

WOW!

In most **prides**, lionesses are the main hunters. Male lions often don't help with hunting.

A **lioness** teaches her cubs to hunt. The lionesses work together. They can catch bigger **prey** by working as a team. They share the meat with their cubs.

Growing Up

Lion **cubs** stay with their mother for a few years. They learn from her. She teaches them how to survive. Then they become adults.

Sometimes young male lions form a group.

Female cubs usually stay with the **pride** when they grow up. Male cubs often have to leave. They may live on their own. They look for a pride to take over.

Starting Again

A young **lioness** can help her **pride**. She hunts with the others. She helps take care of the **cubs**. She helps to protect the pride.

A lioness needs a mate. She chooses one of the pride's male lions.

The young lioness is an adult.
She can have her own cubs.
Soon she will become **pregnant**.
The life cycle has started again.

The Life Cycle

A lioness gives birth to cubs.

The cubs drink milk from their mother. They grow bigger and stronger.

A female cub stays with the pride. She will have her own cubs.

The lioness teaches her cubs to hunt and survive.

Fact File

Average life span: about 10 years in the wild

Size: up to 6.5 feet (2 m) long, not including tail

Weight: up to 420 pounds (190 kg)

Diet: meat (wildebeest, antelope, buffalo, zebra)

WOW!

Lions roar loudly. The noise warns other lion prides to stay away.

Try It!

Make a list of animals that lions eat. Start with the ones mentioned on page 21. Do research to find more animals to add to the list.

Now you can research the prey animals. How big are they? Are they fast runners? Do they have defenses, such as horns? Make notes for each one.

Which animals do you think will be easiest for the lions to catch?

Animal	Size	Fast or slow	Defenses
Antelope	Medium	Fast	Horns
Zebra			
Buffalo			
Wildebeest			

Useful Words

big cat one of the kinds of closely-related large cats. Lions, tigers, jaguars, leopards, and snow leopards are big cats.

cub a young lion

lioness a female lion

litter a group of cubs born to the same mother at the same time

mammal an animal with a body covered in fur, which makes milk to feed its young

mate a partner of the opposite sex that an animal can have babies with

predators animals that catch and eat other animals

pregnant when a female animal has one or more unborn babies inside her body

prey animals that predators hunt for food

pride a group of lions that live together

Find out More

Websites

animals.sandiegozoo.org/animals/lion

www.dkfindout.com/uk/animals-and-nature/cats/lion/

www.natgeokids.com/uk/discover/animals/general-animals/10-lion-facts/

Books

A Pride of Lions Amy Kortuem, Pebble Books 2019

Explore My World: Lions Amy Sky Koster, National Geographic 2018

Lions Claire Archer, Capstone 2016

Index

adults 4, 16, 19

choosing a mate 18

cubs 7, 8, 9, 10, 11, 12, 13, 15, 16, 17, 18, 19

dens 10

eyes 8, 9

hunting 13, 14, 15, 18

learning 9, 13, 16

life cycles 4, 5, 19

mammals 5, 8
meat 14, 15
milk 5, 9, 14
mothers 5, 8, 9, 11, 12, 16

playing 12, 13
predators 10
pride 6, 7, 11, 12, 17, 18